8/14

FIRST AMERICANS
The Inuit

DAVID C. KING

 **Marshall Cavendish**
Benchmark
New York

ACKNOWLEDGMENTS

Series consultant: Raymond Bial

Marshall Cavendish Benchmark
99 White Plains Road
Tarrytown, New York 10591-9001
www.marshallcavendish.us

Text copyright © 2008 by Marshall Cavendish Corp.
Map and illustrations copyright ©2008 by Marshall Cavendish Corp.
Map illustration by Rodica Prato
Craft illustrations by Chris Santoro

All Internet sites were available and accurate when sent to press.

Library of Congress Cataloging-in-Publication Data
King, David C.
  The Inuit / by David C. King
        p. cm. — (First Americans)
  Summary: "Provides comprehensive information on the background, lifestyle, beliefs, and present-day lives of the Inuit people"
—Provided by publisher.
  Includes bibliographical references and index.
  ISBN-13: 978-0-7614-2679-0
 1. Inuit—Juvenile literature. I. Title. II. Series.
  E99.E7K4425 2007
  971.9004'9712—dc22
2006034111

On the cover: An Inuit girl, snug in her fur hood, braves the Alaskan winter.
Title page: An Inuit hunter and his dogsled team cross a frozen sea in Greenland.

Photo research by Connie Gardner
Cover photo by Galen Rowell/CORBIS
The photographs in this book are used by permission and through the courtesy of: Corbis: Layne Kennedy, 1; Darrel Gulin, 4; Wolfgang Kaehler, 12; Stapleton Collection, 17; Michael Maslan Historic Photographs, 27; Joshua Strang/US Airforce/ZUMA, 30; DK Limited, 37. The Granger Collection: 7, 29; NorthWind Picture Archive: 8, 21; Art Resource: Werner Forman, 10,22,23; Nativestock.com: Marilyn "Angel" Wynn, 14, 16, 20, 24; Getty Images: Andre Forget/AFP, 12; America 24–7, 35, Chris Arend/Stone, 40.

Editor: Deborah Grahame
Publisher: Michelle Bisson
Art Director: Anahid Hamparian
Series designer: Symon Chow

Printed in China
1 3 5 6 4 2

CONTENTS

1 · THE PEOPLE OF THE MIDNIGHT SUN

The Inuit (IN-yoo-it) live in one of the world's harshest environments. Their frozen Arctic home stretches from Alaska and the islands of the Bering Sea in the west, across Canada to the coast of Greenland in the east, covering about 6,000 miles (9,656 kilometers). This frozen land is sometimes called the "Land of the Midnight Sun," because, at the North Pole, the sun never really sets between March 20 and September 22.

The word *Inuit* means "the people." The Inuit were once known as *Eskimos*, a term the Inuit did not like because it comes from a Cree Indian word meaning "eaters of raw meat."

Although the Inuit enjoy the long daylight in summer, their land is dark and cold much of the year, with temperatures averaging between –20 and –30 degrees Fahrenheit (between –29 and –34 degrees Celsius). Their small villages

A summer sunset glows on the Alaska Range.

Inuit homelands cover Arctic areas in Alaska, Canada, Greenland, and Russian Siberia.

are clustered at the edge of the sea, with a flat grassland called **tundra** behind them. For three to four months of the year, the upper few inches of tundra thaws, and the coastal plain suddenly comes alive with color as flowers and bushes burst into bloom. For a few weeks, berries provide a bit of variety in the Inuit diet. Below the upper few inches of soil is **permafrost** that never thaws.

The Inuit of long ago had skills that helped them survive in the frigid Arctic north. They hunted sea mammals, especially seals, and off the coast of Alaska they hunted whales and

An engraving of an Inuit hunter equipped with bow and arrows, snowshoes, and his dog.

A nineteenth-century woodcut shows the Inuit herding caribou (reindeer) into a corral.

walruses. Several kinds of fish, as well as migratory birds such as geese and ducks, were also part of their diet. Sometimes they also hunted polar bears and caribou (reindeer).

These animals provided everything the Inuit needed to survive and to prosper in a harsh climate. Oil from sea mammals, especially whales, gave the Inuit fuel for cooking and for oil lamps. Clothing was made from the skin and fur, while tools were made from bones and rocks.

Thousands of years ago, the first of the Native Americans came across a land bridge that connected eastern Asia (Siberia) with western North America (Alaska). Long after the Native Americans spread through North and South America, the ocean level rose and the land bridge disappeared.

Did the first Inuit cross from Asia to Alaska before the Bering Sea covered the land bridge, or did they come later in large animal-skin boats called **umiaks**? No one knows for certain. Scientists do know, however, that the Inuit were the last people to cross from Asia. Physically, they looked more like the people of modern Mongolia than the other Native Americans.

From coastal Alaska, the Inuit gradually moved eastward in search of new hunting grounds. In the easternmost regions of Inuit settlement—Labrador and Greenland—the first

This model of an umiak shows a helmsman and his rowers manning the oars.

contacts with Europeans were made when fishermen from Norway arrived around 1000 CE. These small settlements disappeared by the late 1300s and had no lasting effect on Inuit life.

More frequent contact began when European explorers arrived in the sixteenth and seventeenth centuries. These explorers sailed through the Arctic Sea, looking for a sea route through North America to the Pacific Ocean. The 1700s also brought American whaling ships to the area. The explorers and whalers often spent winter with the Inuit.

The Inuit enjoyed trading with the Europeans and Americans, and they liked hearing about Europe and the United States. These outsiders, however, brought diseases new to the Inuit. Smallpox alone claimed thousands of lives, sometimes wiping out entire villages. By the late 1800s the Inuit population had been reduced by about two-thirds.

The Americans and Europeans encouraged the Inuit to trade furs for manufactured goods, including rifles. Inuit hunters eagerly brought furs to trading posts in Alaska and Canada. Modern weapons, such as steel harpoons and rifles, enabled the Inuit to collect and trade more furs. By the early 1900s the populations of sea mammals and caribou had

A carving of a walrus features tusks made of ivory.

declined. The Inuit had less to trade, but they now depended on American and European goods. To reduce suffering, the U.S. and Canadian governments provided food, shelter, and medical care. Through much of the twentieth century, the Inuit found themselves caught between two worlds. Their traditional way of life could no longer support them, but the Americans and Canadians had few jobs to offer. As a result, many Inuit families lived in poverty.

By the second half of the twentieth century, nearly all of the Inuit had been forced to give up their traditional way of life. They lived in wood-frame houses, dressed in modern clothing, and sent their children to public schools. In spite of the hardships they faced, the Inuit maintained some of their traditions. They kept their own language, called **Inuktitut**. They continued to pass on their history through storytelling, and they practiced traditional arts, including carvings made out of **soapstone** or walrus tusks.

2 · THE INUIT WAY OF LIFE

In spring, behind the Inuit's coastal villages, the top few inches of the tundra thawed. Flowers and shrubs bloomed. Soon the women and girls would be filling sealskin bags with sweet berries.

This was also the time of year for the whale hunt. The bowhead (or polar) whale arrived at its summer feeding grounds in the Arctic Ocean. Inuit men prepared for the hunt in groups of five or six. Every group had a large skin-covered umiak. Each umiak owner made sure that his men had new clothing and weapons, and that everyone had several sacred objects to ensure a good hunt.

At other times the Inuit often joked, laughed, and sang. This was a serious occasion, and the men were silent.

When they saw a whale, the men sprang into action. They

Springtime in the Alaskan tundra

paddled hard, singing sacred songs as they went. In the prow, the harpooner made sure his weapons were ready. The harpoon was a complex tool with a detachable head and sturdy rope. At exactly the right moment, while singing his own song, the harpooner let the harpoon fly, burying it deep in the whale's body. He then attacked with spears, and the Inuit got their whale.

A harpooner stands beside his one-person boat.

A successful hunt was a joyous event, because the danger of hunger and even starvation was always present. Men in several umiaks towed a whale carcass to shore. The Inuit sang and laughed as the big animal was butchered. Meat and blubber from each whale were distributed to every household.

The Inuit also hunted walruses and seals. The best technique was to find the mammal's breathing hole, or *aglu*, in the ice. Hunters had to remain still and wait patiently for many hours before a seal appeared. When a seal or walrus came up for air, the hunter struck fast with a spear. Hunters

An Inuit hunter patiently watches a seal's breathing hole.

often worked alone, traveling in one-person boats called *qajaqs*, which Americans referred to as **kayaks**. Like the larger umiaks, the kayaks were made of sealskin stretched across a frame of animal bones.

Whale and seal meat, mixed with blubber, were the Inuit's staple foods. They provided good nutrition, and the fat was essential protection against the cold. This diet was supplemented by fish, caribou meat, and birds.

The Inuit often ate raw meat, although women sometimes boiled it in bowls made of soapstone, into which they dropped hot rocks. The Inuit ate partly digested seaweed or shrimp from the stomachs of seals and blood soup. In addition to berries, summer foods included roots and seaweed. A special treat for children was a mixture of berries and blubber.

There were no set mealtimes. The Inuit ate whenever they were hungry. A person would cut off a piece of meat then hold it in his or her teeth in order to slice off bite-size pieces. Meals were different after a successful whale hunt, when everyone ate until they were full.

Inuit Fish Soup

The Inuit would have made this soup without the tomatoes, onions, olive oil, and parsley, but we have added them for flavor. The Inuit traditionally flavored food with fat and sauces. You will need these ingredients:

- 2 medium-sized onions
- measuring spoons
- 2 tablespoons olive oil
- cutting board
- a sprig of fresh parsley or 2 teaspoons of dried parsley
- paring knife
- stew or soup pot, with lid

- 4 tomatoes
- large mixing spoon
- 2 pounds cod, haddock, or other firm fish
- adult helper
- water
- 1 teaspoon salt
- 1 teaspoon pepper

Makes 4 servings

1. With an adult's help, peel the onions and chop them into small pieces, and chop up the parsley.
2. Cut the tomatoes into small pieces.
3. Remove skin and bones from the fish, and cut the meat into chunks. Put the olive oil in the soup pot. Sauté the onions over medium heat until they are golden brown (about 5 minutes). Add the parsley.
4. Add the tomatoes and fish, then add enough water to barely cover the ingredients.
5. Cover and cook over medium heat for about 20 minutes.
6. Sprinkle with salt and pepper. Serve hot.

Several families usually lived close together, and everyone moved when it was time to find new sources of food. Although the Inuit moved around a lot, they rarely traveled very far. In fact, they could name every rock, hill, and inlet within their territory.

In winter most Inuit lived in **karmats**, square or rectangular houses built over a shallow pit, then covered with sod. The frame was made of wood or whale bone. Some Inuit lived in temporary shelters made of hard-packed snow called **igloos**. The snow was cut in blocks and stacked into a dome shape. Lamps fueled by seal oil were used to heat the inside air. This melted some of the inside snow, which refroze and created an insulating layer of ice. A long,

The entrance to an Inuit sod-covered dwelling

An Inuit igloo village during seal-hunting season

low entranceway kept out the wind and cold, keeping the interior warm. On the inside, a low bench of packed snow stretched around three sides of the structure. This bench was covered with skins and furs. It was used as a sleeping bench at night and as a working area during the day. During summer the Inuit lived in tents made of sealskin stretched over frames of bones and driftwood.

In the cold climate of the Arctic, the Inuit needed warm

clothing to survive. Women were highly skilled in the design and making of clothes. The pullover parka with an attached hood was their most essential garment, along with trousers and waterproof boots. The parka and trousers were made of two layers of skins placed back to back, with a fur layer on the outside and a finer fur (usually caribou) on the inside, against the wearer's skin. The outer layer of skins was coated regularly with fish oil to keep it water-resistant. Women's parkas, especially the hood, were made extra large so they could carry infants snugly on their backs.

For transportation on land, the Inuit relied on dogsleds. Made of bone and driftwood, the sleds were 15 to 30 feet (4.5 to 9 meters) long. Six to twelve huskies, the Inuit breed of dogs, pulled each sled. On narrow

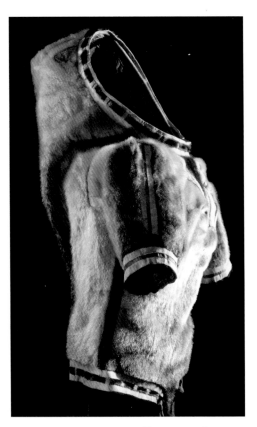

A woman's pullover parka

trails, the dogs were harnessed in single file, with the strongest dog in front. In more open and rugged terrain, they were harnessed in a fan shape, so each dog could find its own footing. Each husky required about one pound (.45 kilograms) of meat a day, plus a quarter pound

A very small Inuit sled made of wood

(.11 kg) of fat. When necessary, though, they could travel for several days without food.

Families were closely knit, and children were treated with love and respect. A child was almost never punished, since children were well aware of how they should behave.

In spite of the harsh environment, the Inuit were a cheerful, fun-loving people. In the evening, especially during winter, they sang, told stories or jokes, and played games.

3 · INUIT BELIEFS

The Inuit lived as a part of nature, so it is not surprising that their religion was closely connected to the natural world. Their religious beliefs were woven into the fabric of their daily lives.

The Inuit believed that every living creature had a soul. They had great respect for all animals, but especially for the ones they hunted. They believed that these animals were superior to humans. The animals allowed themselves to be hunted, either because they felt sorry for the humans or because Inuit rituals gave the hunters temporary control.

The hunters showed their respect for animals throughout the hunt and afterward. The boat leader sang songs and made sure all his men had new or freshly cleaned equipment. During a whale hunt he also offered the whale fresh water

Everything in nature was part of the Inuit's religious beliefs.

because salt water made it thirsty. After the hunt, certain songs and rituals were used to thank the animal's spirit.

Inuit beliefs gave them certain ways to protect themselves. Every individual had many **amulets** such as an eagle's claw, a small tree branch, a seashell, or some other object intended to bring good luck or to ward off evil. The Inuit placed amulets on tents, tools, kayaks, harnesses, and clothing. The loss of an amulet was a disaster.

The Inuit believed that taboos—strict rules of things to avoid—also protected them. Seal and caribou were not to be hunted on the same day, for example, nor should the meat of both animals be eaten on the same day. Violating a taboo could lead to an unsuccessful hunt or illness.

Some Inuit, known as **shamans**, were believed to have special powers. They were called on to cure certain illnesses or injuries. Every person was believed to have several souls. Illness or injury meant that one of the souls had left the person's body. The shaman's job was to coax it back with special songs, prayers, and rituals.

A shaman, or medicine man, drives out the evil spirits that made this boy ill.

Women who were giving birth lived apart from the rest of the household. In most communities a special birthing hut was used, and the women remained there with the newborn infant for several days. During the first two years of life, children spent much of their time inside their mother's parka. The Inuit used moss for diapers.

Unlike many other Native American tribes of North America, the Inuit had no special coming of age rituals. A girl might have her chin tattooed to

Inuit Creation Myths

Among the Inuit's many myths, two deal with the creation of life. The Alaska Inuit have myths about Raven, a supernatural bird that had all the qualities of humans. Many myths mention Raven the Trickster, who found clever ways to outsmart other creatures. In one myth, Raven brought the world into existence by harpooning the land from his kayak. This made the earth stable so life could begin.

The Inuit who live farther east had a different creation myth. It involved Sedna, the Lady of the Sea. In this story, the earth was once inhabited by giants, including Sedna and her parents. After a quarrel, her parents tried to put Sedna in the icy waters of the sea, but she reached up and held back their canoe. To escape, the parents chopped off her fingers. One by one, the fingers turned into animals of the sea—whales, walruses, seals, salmon, and others. Sedna continues to live at the bottom of the sea. When the Inuit are short of food, they call to Sedna and she supplies what they need.

show that she was ready for marriage. Boys usually had their lips pierced so they could insert decorations called **labrets**.

Marriage was very informal and usually took place as soon as a couple was old enough to have children. There was no formal wedding. The couple simply moved in together.

The division of labor between men and women was essential for survival. Men hunted and made tools and equipment. Women prepared food, stored some of it for winter, made clothing, and cared for the children.

Households often included

An early twentieth-century photo of an Inuit couple

29

Curtains of color shiver above Alaska's Bear Lake.

grandparents. Sometimes grandparents acted as storytellers, entertaining the family and recalling great events in the history of the Inuit.

There were special ceremonies and taboos surrounding death. Usually a member of the family took the body of the deceased far away from the village. They placed some of the dead person's belongings with the body so they could be used in the afterlife. The body was covered with small stones and driftwood and surrounded by a circle of stones. The Inuit watched the **aurora borealis** (northern lights), believing they could see the deceased dancing in the afterlife.

4 · THE PRESENT AND THE FUTURE

In the past, the Inuit faced a challenging life in a harsh environment. New ways of life brought comforts, but also hardships. In the United States, Canada, and Greenland, the Inuit struggled to adjust to major changes while also trying to preserve their traditions.

The Inuit now live in modern houses and in settled villages. They buy clothing from stores and no longer wear garments made of animal skins and furs. The umiak and kayak have largely been replaced by motorboats, and the dogsled has given way to snowmobiles and other motorized vehicles. Rifles have made it easier to hunt.

With modern medical care, people now enjoy much longer lives, and their populations have grown. There are now about 100,000 Inuit in the world's Arctic regions: 34 percent

The modern Inuit village of Iqaluit in Canada

in Alaska, 29 percent in Canada, 36 percent in Greenland, and about 1 percent in Russian Siberia.

After living in poverty for much of the twentieth century, life began to improve for the Inuit after 1970. The governments of the United States, Canada, and Greenland all created programs to improve health care, education, and job opportunities.

Many Alaska Inuit continue to rely on fishing and hunting whales or other animals for food and for furs to sell. Some find work in the oil, mining, and construction industries. But there are still not enough jobs, and unemployment remains a serious problem.

There is great concern over the growing evidence of global warming. The melting of the Arctic ice and glaciers is having a greater impact on the Inuit than on people in other parts of the world.

However, several developments give the Inuit new reasons for hope in the twenty-first century. Government programs

A whale-hunting crew stand by their umiak, waiting for the order to rush to the hunt.

have improved education and, at least in Alaska, the Inuit take the same courses as other children in the United States. At the same time, they learn traditional crafts and the Inuit language.

Another positive sign has been the decision of the U.S.

Inuktitut: The Inuit Language

Although the Inuit were spread over a 5,000-mile (8,000-km) area from Alaska to Greenland, most Inuit communities could understand each other. They created many of their words by adding one or more prefixes to a basic root word. For example, the Inuktitut word *igdlo* means "house." With *igdlo* as a root word, the Inuit could form one long word with many syllables, such as *igdlorssualiorpoq*, which means "he who builds a large house." People often say that the Inuit have dozens of words for "snow." This is actually an example of the Inuit practice of adding on to root words. In this way, different words can be formed to describe different kinds of snow or different activities relating to snow.

Some combination words can be very short, like *Ikkiirnaqtuq* ("It is cold"). Many Inuit words stand alone, unless they become a root word to build on. Here are some examples:

ujaraq	rock	*tupiq*	tent
nanuq	polar bear	*qanniq*	falling snow
nasak	hat or hood	*qajaq*	kayak
aput	snow		

Congress to award nearly $1 billion and 44 million acres (18 million hectares) of land to the native peoples of Alaska. In Canada, government programs have led to the creation of entire towns with low-cost housing. In 1999 Canada established a large territory where mostly Inuit people live. This territory, called Nunavut, covers much of northern Canada.

Traditional skills, such as soapstone carving, sculpting in ivory or bone, printmaking, and **scrimshaw** have provided new sources of income. Local cooperatives offer grants or loans, work space, training, and marketing for Inuit artists and craftspeople, who have found a growing demand for their work.

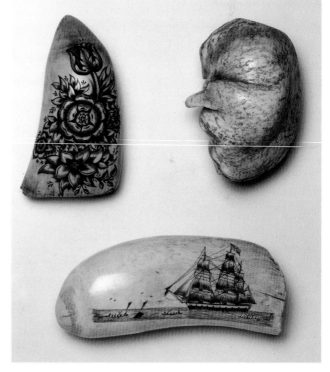

Scrimshaw carvings on whale bones

Inuit Soapstone Carving

In the past, the Inuit made small carvings out of bone or walrus tusks. These were simple animal forms that they hoped would bring them good luck in hunting. In the late nineteenth century, as ivory became scarce, they began to carve soapstone instead. Soapstone carvings have become highly valued. Many pieces are displayed in museums around the world.

For your soapstone carving you will use a bar of soft soap, such as Ivory, or self-hardening modeling clay.

Ask an adult to supervise this activity.

You will need:

- a bar of soft soap
  (or a package self-hardening clay)
- pencil and scrap paper
- plastic knife or table knife
  (a paring or pen knife can be used
  with an adult's help)
- modeling tools (optional)
- sponge

1· Sketch an animal on a piece of scrap paper. A rounded form is best, such as a polar bear, whale, rabbit, or cat. Keep it simple, and try sketching the front and back, as well as the side.

2· Copy your drawing onto the bar of soap or clay.

3· Hold the soap or clay in one hand. Hold the knife in your other hand and press your thumb against the bottom of the bar, cutting slowly toward your thumb. Take off only thin slivers with each stroke.

4· Use the pencil or modeling tools to add details or texture.

5· When you have cut out the basic shape, scrape the surface with your knife to smooth it. For an even smoother surface, wet a sponge and wipe the sculpture gently. Allow it to dry.

The traditional "blanket toss" is popular at Inuit gatherings.

Government programs have also encouraged other ways to make traditional Inuit pursuits profitable. In Greenland, for example, many Inuit have turned to commercial fishing and have formed several successful companies.

In Alaska, tourism has become very popular. The Alaska Inuit have even managed to continue hunting whales. Although there is a strong movement to ban whaling, the International Whaling Commission continues to permit a limited Inuit harvest each year.

Every two years since 1970, the Inuit of Alaska, Canada, and Greenland have staged the Arctic Winter Games, featuring various traditional games, such as kayak and dogsled races. Art and culture also receive recognition. In 2006 Cape Dorset in Nunavut was voted the most artistic city in Canada. These are signs of progress that continue to boost hopes for the future of the Inuit people.

· TIME LINE

People begin to cross the Bering Sea land bridge connecting Asia (Siberia) and North America (Alaska).

Ice Age ends; ancestors of Inuit cross to Alaska by boat.

Inuit groups move eastward, starting new settlements across northern Canada to Labrador and Greenland.

Inuit encounter Norse fishing villages in Labrador.

Explorers searching for a Northwest Passage meet Inuit; American whalers reach Arctic Ocean; crews often winter with Inuit; diseases kill more than half the Inuit people.

Traditional hunting and fishing no longer support the people; Inuit become dependent on government aid, but many live in poverty.

Congress passes a law making all Native Americans citizens of the United States.

40,000 BCE -6000 CE

6000 BCE

4000 BCE -1000 CE

1000 CE

1600-1800 CE

Early 1900s

1924

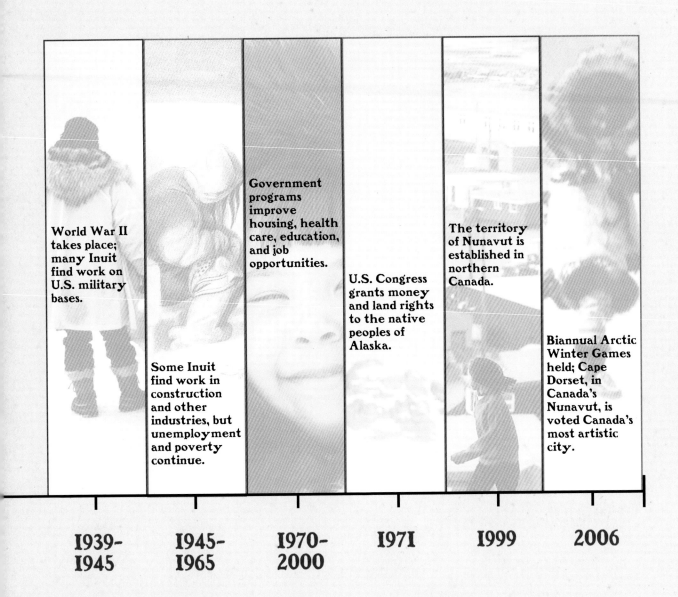

World War II takes place; many Inuit find work on U.S. military bases.

Some Inuit find work in construction and other industries, but unemployment and poverty continue.

Government programs improve housing, health care, education, and job opportunities.

U.S. Congress grants money and land rights to the native peoples of Alaska.

The territory of Nunavut is established in northern Canada.

Biannual Arctic Winter Games held; Cape Dorset, in Canada's Nunavut, is voted Canada's most artistic city.

1939-1945

1945-1965

1970-2000

1971

1999

2006

· GLOSSARY

amulets: Sacred objects designed to bring good luck or ward off bad luck.

aurora borealis: Moving ribbons of light seen above the Arctic Circle caused by electrically charged particles from the sun colliding with oxygen and nitrogen in the earth's atmosphere.

igloos: Dome-shaped houses made of blocks of snow.

Inuktitut: The Inuit language.

karmats: Square or rectangular houses built by the Inuit, especially those living in Alaska and Greenland.

kayaks: Narrow one-person boats made of animal skins stretched over a frame made of bone or driftwood.

labrets: Ornaments made of bone worn by men as a piercing in the lower lip.

permafrost: A layer of soil that is permanently frozen.

scrimshaw: Art form made by scratching images in bone or ivory and then darkening the lines. The craft was invented by American whalers in the early 1800s.

shaman: A Native American healer believed to have skills that allow him or her to understand and heal some illnesses and injuries.

soapstone: A soft stone used for carving small sculptures and various household utensils.

tundra: Treeless land in Arctic regions. Only a few inches thaw at the surface for a few weeks every summer; the land underneath is permanently frozen.

umiaks: Large skin-covered boats used to move people and goods, or to hunt for large sea animals, especially whales.

· FIND OUT MORE

Books

Bial, Raymond. *The Inuit*. New York: Marshall Cavendish, 2002.

Cordoba, Yasmine. *Igloo.* Vero Beach, FL: Rourke Publications Inc., 2001.

Corriveau, Danielle. *The Inuit of Canada*. Minneapolis, MN: Lerner Publications, 2002.

Santella, Andrew. *The Inuit*. Danbury, CT: Children's Press, 2001.

Web Sites

Government of Nunavut
www.gov.nu.ca/Nunavut

Inuit Art Foundation

www.inuitart.org

Inuit History for Kids

www.historyforkids.org/learn/northamerica/before1500/
history/inuit.htm

Nunavut Parks

www.nunavutparks.com/index.cfm

About the Author

David C. King is an award-winning author who has written more than seventy books for children and young adults, including *The Navajo*, *The Nez Perce*, and *The Sioux* in the First Americans series. He and his wife, Sharon, live in the Berkshires at the junction of New York, Massachusetts, and Connecticut. Their travels have taken them through most of the United States.

· INDEX

Page numbers in **boldface** are illustrations.